THE CHINA PAINTER INSTRUCTION BOOK

LECTOR HOUSE PUBLIC DOMAIN WORKS

HAPPY READING!

THE CHINA PAINTER INSTRUCTION BOOK

ANONYMOUS

ISBN: 978-93-5614-231-2

Published: -

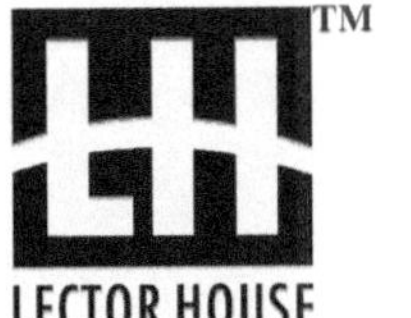

LECTOR HOUSE LLP
E-MAIL: lectorpublishing@gmail.com

THE CHINA PAINTER INSTRUCTION BOOK

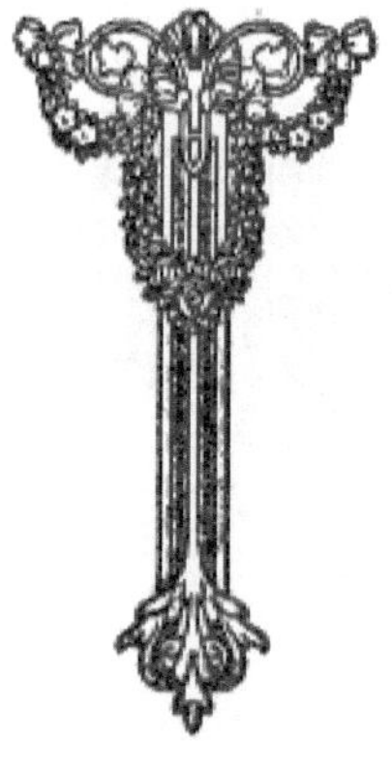

[SECOND EDITION]

CONTENTS

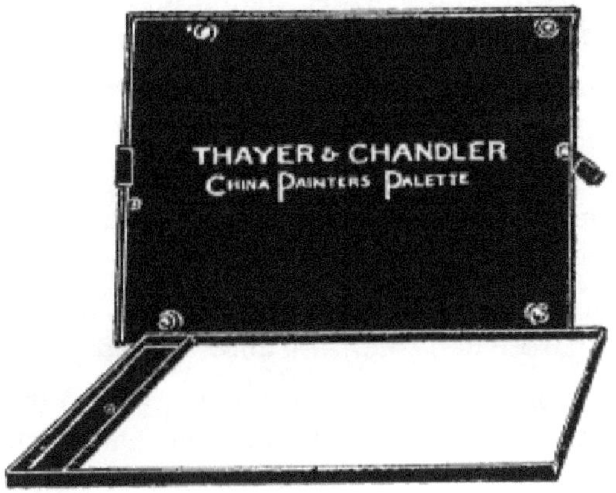

MIXING OF THE CHINA COLORS

There are many things of which the beginner in china painting should be reminded. It is most essential that he has clean tools and well mixed colors before attempting any work. To be sure poorly ground colors are more quickly and more easily prepared, but nothing but the very poorest results can be obtained from such haste.

After placing a small quantity of powder color on a clean slab and enough mixing medium to make a thick paste, blend the two together with a small palette knife, working with a rotary motion. See well to it that no particles are left. When blending, keep the palette knife as flat as possible, as there is danger of breaking it if bent too much. Mix well until the color is a smooth paste. It will be found well to put a small amount of the mixing medium in a small dish and use from that, rather than pouring it from bottle.

When thoroughly mixed, put the color on one side of the palette. Blend another color and place next to the other one on the palette. Proceed in this way until all the tints wanted are prepared. It will be found that some colors take longer than others to grind, owing to their stony nature. In this case a little patience is necessary for best results.

Have a clean cup of turpentine and a small dish with a few drops of light working medium at hand. Use a clean, square brush. Take the color desired, rub down on the palette so as to have all of the brush moist with it, and apply to the china, of course it is understood that before beginning the work, the design has been carefully drawn on the china, either with a wax pencil or India ink and pen. This drawing will disappear in firing.

If the design is carefully drawn on the china, it will assist the decorator in easily placing the tints where they belong.

Wash your brush in turpentine, when changing colors, and be sure to press the turpentine out with a cloth before dipping the brush into another color.

Care should be taken to see that all colors are applied evenly, always using the brush flat.

Never hesitate to erase the design and repaint the china, in case it is not entirely satisfactory. This may seem a little discouraging but the result will reward one for the additional labor.

It is very necessary to clean all brushes and palettes used, when through working. Brushes become hard when colors are allowed to dry in them.

Throughout this work we devote special chapters to the various features of china painting such as lining, mixing of colors, etc., and with this lesson we feel that the beginner has a fair start; she will soon learn what the different combinations of colors will produce. For instance, blue and purple or blue and ruby make violet. Blue and yellow make a green, green and a little black make gray, reds mixed with black make brown. Do not mix lustre colors as results will not be satisfactory.

COLOR COMBINATIONS

One feature of china painting that requires much study and consideration is the combining of colors. A design that would be most attractive if the colorings harmonized, would be almost a failure otherwise. Browns go well with nearly all colors, but not as well with greens and blues as with some others. Clear blues, with perhaps the exception of the darkest blues and Copenhagen, are not very satisfactory for borders. A border of this combination, however, is very effective. A beautiful shade can be produced by combining yellow brown, finishing brown, ivory yellow and just a little touch of gold.

Violet of iron and auburn brown on a grayish ground, combine very well.

Pearl gray with Copenhagen blue gives a soft effect. Ivory goes well with yellow-greens, and violets with grayish tones.

A piece of china done in yellow tones, with say a conventional motif decoration, or yellow flowers, looks well with a scroll of gold worked into it, and should have a yellow background. If delicate effects are desired, yellow cannot be used successfully. For soft backgrounds, auburn brown, violet of iron, new green, olive green and Copenhagen blue are very good.

A design in gold on a broad border of Copenhagen is both beautiful and effective. There are few decorations stronger than this. For Turkish effects peacock and Sultan green are used principally. A little yellow, green, blue, black, red and dark brown can be used with success in this style of decoration.

A design in silver is very attractive on either a dark gray or green decoration.

Strong and decided contrast in colors, almost always produces pleasing results. Among the best are black and yellow, black and red and black and yellow-green. Rose and red do not go well together. Neither does blue or blue-green go well with red, but red and olive green contrast well. For a beautiful dark blue, mix banding blue with about one-fifth part of hair black. Ivory yellow or light green look well on a dark green band, and gold on maroon. To produce a good maroon use ruby purple and one-sixth part of peacock green.

A very beautiful color that we can hardly name, comes from mixing three parts of peacock green with one part of crimson purple. The result is about a deep steel blue.

If a dark green ground is treated with ruby or crimson purple, before the second firing, it produces a very warm effect.

Combine one-fourth of Russian green with Copenhagen blue and you have dark gray.

Yellows destroy red and should never be mixed.

A very delicate blue-gray can be produced by mixing turquoise blue and about one-sixth of black. Use more or less of black as desired.

Violet and brown makes a striking color. A light wash of hair brown or Meissen produces a tan.

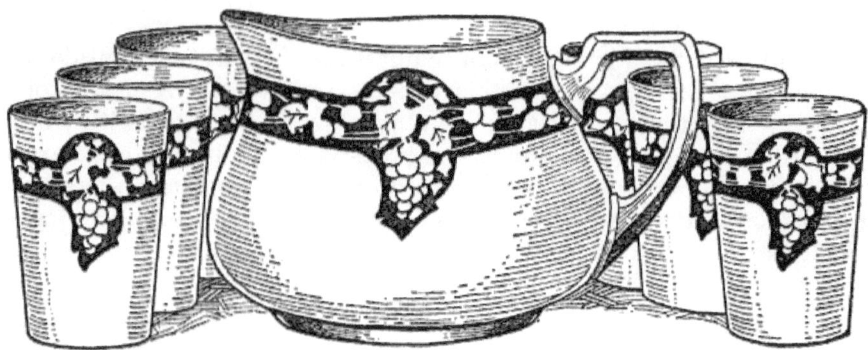

CONVENTIONAL STYLE PAINTING

The old-fashioned naturalistic style of china decoration is a thing of the past. One sees almost nothing of that sort in the metropolitan exhibitions, because patrons of Keramic art are weary of a type which admits of so little variety and individuality.

Flowers and fruit have gradually been shaped into designs, and these in many cases are so conventionalized that they have lost almost all resemblance to the original form.

There can be no doubt that conventional work has come to stay, and there is a distinct gain in this. Endless opportunities are opened for the artist to show character in both composition and color.

The china painter of yesterday spent her time almost entirely on color. The natural flowers were often placed almost anywhere on the china and were admired for color and treatment alone.

No wonder Keramics was not considered an art!

To-day the artist *thinks* before she touches the color work.

A design should suggest the shape to which it is to be applied, and proportion plays an important part. A plate, for instance, with too wide a band is a pitiful thing, and a design that is not properly bound together is to be shunned.

A low stocky looking piece may be treated with a motif used once on either side and connected with a gold or color band. It is a common mistake to try to bind the body of a teapot, or similar article, and the spout and handle! The two latter are entirely separate and demand other treatment.

Plenty of plain background will enhance the effect of the design. One can easily overload a piece of china with a design good in itself but too elaborate and large.

The first law of conventional design is that each form must be outlined. When this is done the decorator should have a comparatively easy time, and a remarkably interesting one, for conventional work is adapted especially to wonderful color combinations.

The colors, as a rule, are more effective when laid on in flat tones. Shading is not at all common in strictly conventional work, and one does not necessarily adhere to the colors nature has chosen for the object which suggested the design.

Enamel and lustre are especially fitting to conventional design, and gold may often be used for flower or leaf form where in naturalistic painting it would be entirely out of place.

For a long time keramic artists looked askance at the new style because of the amount of work required in outlining. This was a tedious affair involving a fine brush or pen, paint or ink, which refused to work right, and endless endurance.

All this has been overcome by means of new process outline designs which fire into the china distinctly and form a black outline around the painting. Those who are ambitious may now make a reputation without ruining their eyesight or taxing their patience.

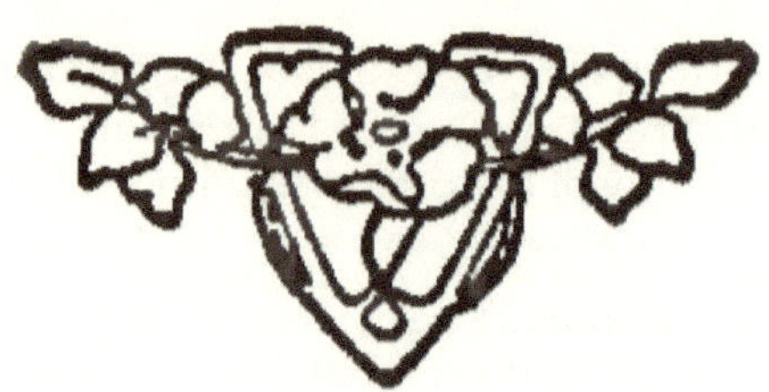

Conventional Single Yellow Rose. Primrose Yellow shaded with Apple Green toward centre; stamens may be Gold or Dark Brown. Light leaves are painted with Moss Green shaded with Shading Green and dark leaves may be laid in with a mixture of Apple Green and a very little Deep Purple. Stems are painted with Auburn Brown. A good background for this scheme is Gray Green lightly applied.

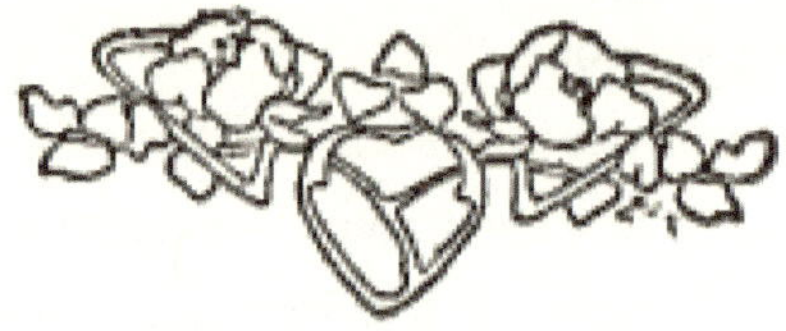

Conventional Wild Rose. Paint with Sweet Pea Pink with very delicate application of Apple Green toward centre. Stamens are painted with Ruby and center dot may be Gold. Leaves are laid in with a mixture of Apple Green and very little Deep Purple. Roman Gold or Turquoise Lustre is effective as a background for inside if design will admit. For outside of design, or general background, use Oriental Ivory.

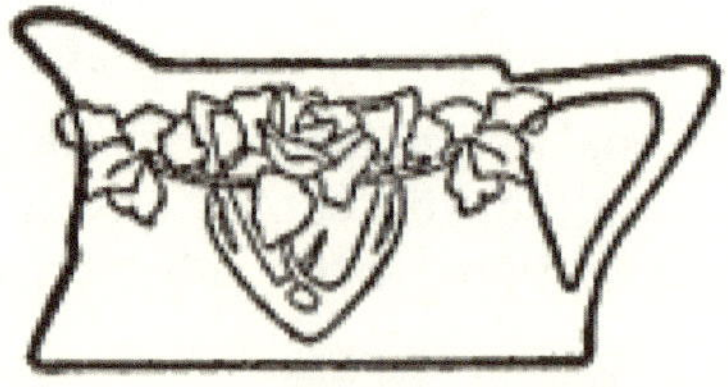

Conventional Double Pink Rose. Use Sweet Pea Pink and shade with Standard Pink in centre. A very pleasing color scheme for leaves is Yellow Green Lustre shaded with Dark Green Lustre. A Pearl Gray background is suitable for this combination.

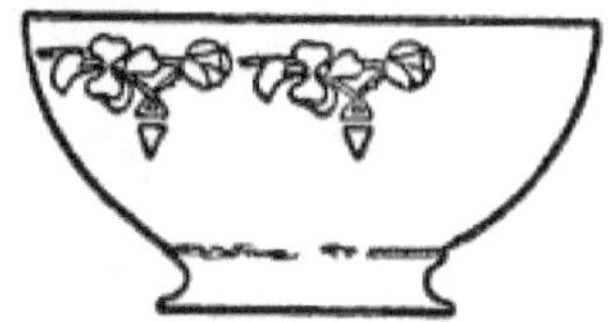

Conventional Rose. These may be treated in either Lustre colors or regular powder colors. A suitable color treatment for lustre decoration is as follows: Lay in a flat wash of Orange or Yellow-Brown Lustre except in centre, this may be Gold. For leaves use a wash of Light Green and shade with Dark Green Lustre. Stems may be Brown or Dark Green. Mother of Pearl is a suitable background for this treatment. For regular powder color treatment, apply thin wash of Sweet Pea Pink with a touch of Standard Pink in centre. Leaves may be painted in with Apple Green shaded with Shading Green. Stems may be Auburn Brown or Apple Green mixed with just a touch of Deep Purple. Oriental Ivory or Gray for Flesh is suitable for background. Either tint will harmonize. The color for roses can be varied to suit individual taste. Primrose Yellow, Blood Red and Rose are all suitable colors.

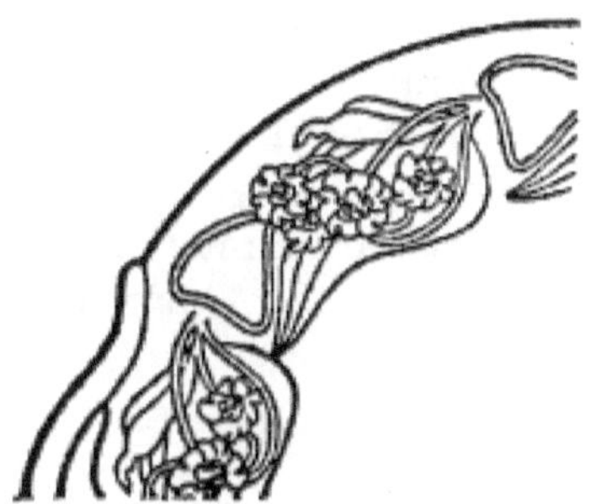

Conventional White Primrose. Let the plain White China answer as white flowers, touch centres with Pompadour. Stamens may be of Gold. A good background for such a color scheme is Pompadour with a touch of Albert Yellow, and Sea Green with a touch of Black mixed with it. Standard Pink, Primrose Yellow, Violet and Blood Red may be used for the flowers if preferred. If bright colors are used, keep background toned down with Gray.

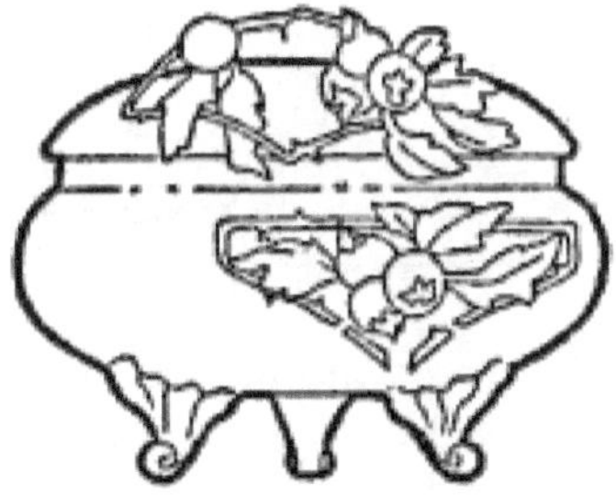

Conventional Hawthorne Berry. For berry, use a mixture of Standard Pink and Yellow Red. Centre may be Black. Leaves should be painted with Moss Green shaded with Shading Green or Apple Green mixed with just a little Deep Purple. Auburn Brown can be used for stems. A flat band to harmonize with such decorations may be laid in with a mixture of Empire Green and Russian Green. Hawthorne berries and leaves may be treated in Lustres as follows: Berries, Silver Lustre centres shaded with Dark Green Lustre. Background, Mother of Pearl Lustre.

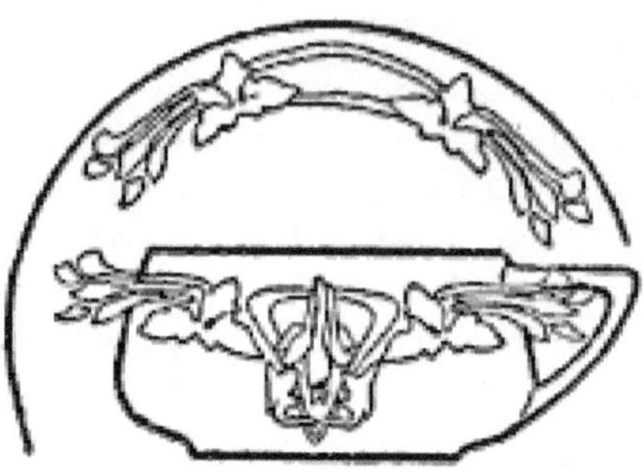

Conventional Columbine. The colors of this flower are so varied so we will of necessity treat only a few. Banding Blue (pale) or Sevres Blue are both very suitable for Blue tints, Primrose Yellow and Albert Yellow tints. Rose, Sweet Pea Pink for Pink tints, and Violet for Violet tints. A very light application of Violet should be applied for light tones and a mixture of Violet and a little Banding Blue for darker tones. Use Best Black for stamens. Leaves are laid in with a light wash of Apple Green and shaded with Shading Green. Gray Green and Oriental Ivory are both suitable for backgrounds. Combinations of Violet Lustre and Mother of Pearl Lustre are also effective for background tinting.

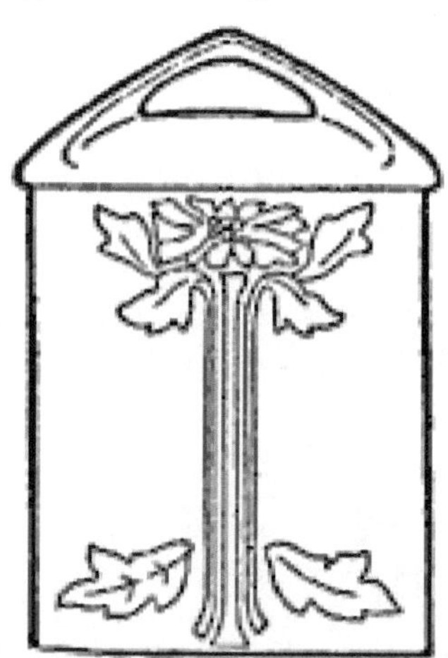

Conventional Poinsettia. Flower should be laid in with Yellow Red shaded with Blood Red toward centre; Yellow Brown is used for stamens. Leaves are painted with Moss Green or Yellow Green shaded with a mixture of Apple Green and very little Deep Purple or Shading Green. Copenhagen Blue may also be used for leaves in extreme shadow.

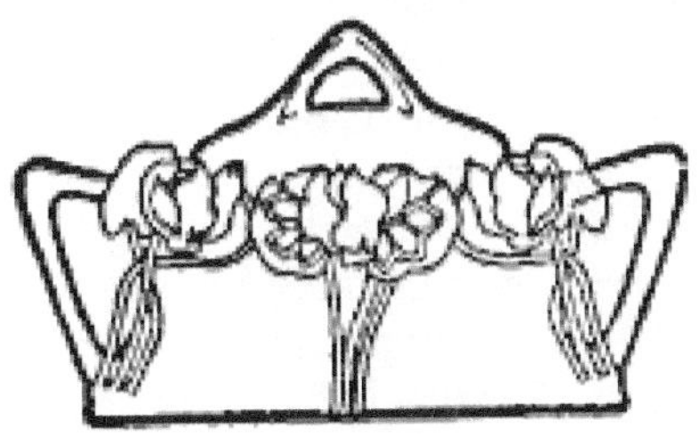

Conventional Cyclamen. Apply a wash of Standard Pink for flowers. Blood Red may be used for Deep Red effects. Leaves may be painted with a mixture of Apple Green and a touch of Deep Purple or with clear Olive Green. Background for this combination may be Roman Purple or Violet Lustre. For yellow flowers use Primrose Yellow mixed with Albert Yellow, with back petals of pale Meissen Brown. Leaves may be laid in with Moss Green and stems with Shading Green. Roman Gold makes an effective background for above the design and Oriental Ivory for below.

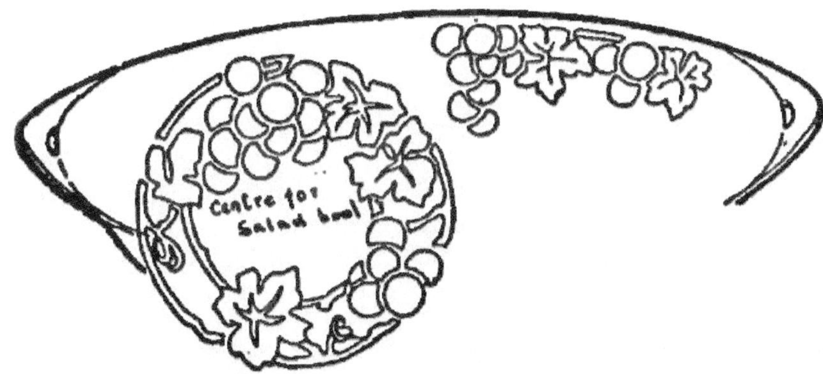

Conventional Grapes. A light wash of Roman Purple should be used for large berries and darker application for smaller berries. Silver Lustre may be used for small berries at the bottom of cluster. To work up the design in semi-lustre effect, Silver Lustre may be used for leaves, and stems laid in with Black. Royal Copenhagen Gray background.

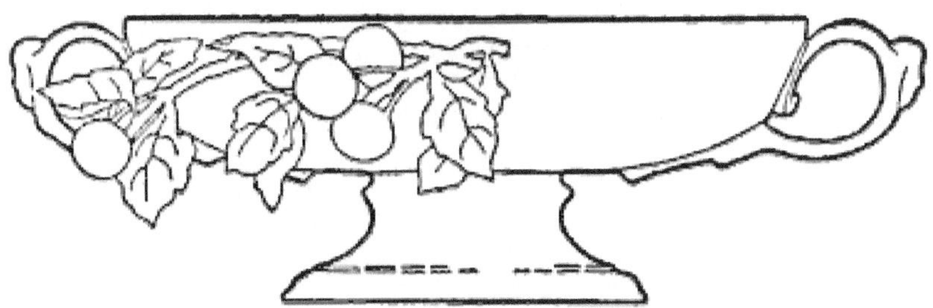

Conventional Apples. Apply wash of Primrose Yellow, shade with Yellow Red. Another effective combination is Yellow Red shaded with Blood Red. Leaves may be painted Moss Green shaded with Shading Green. Stems should be painted with Auburn Brown. For background use Copenhagen Gray, shaded into pale Violet mixed with a touch of Black. A very pretty lustre effect is to lay in some of the fruit with Orange Lustre and others in Roman Gold. The leaves may be painted with both Lustre and painting Tints—some may be Orange Lustre and others Meissen Brown color. Stems should be Auburn Brown. An artistic background would be either clear Oriental Ivory or Oriental Ivory mixed with a touch of Black. It must be borne in mind that these color schemes are intended to be used strictly in connection with conventional New Process Black Outline designs. They are not intended as suggestions for natural style painting. It is not advisable to make use of these instructions unless in connection with black outlines.

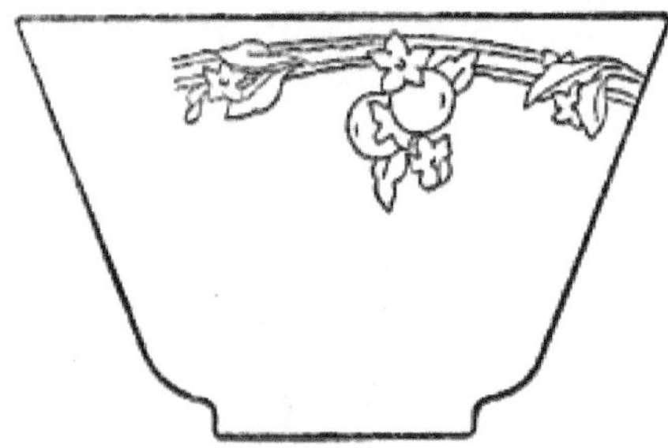

Conventional Oranges. An appropriate conventional style decoration for oranges would be to lay in the foremost one in Roman Gold and those showing only partially in Yellow Brown Lustre. The flowers may be left plain White with touch of Gold in centre. Use Green Lustre for leaves and Dark Empire Green and Auburn Brown may be used for stems. In background of Celestial Turquoise put in a few touches of Meissen Brown next to fruit and under leaves. Warm Gray or Oriental Ivory with touch of Black mixed with it may also be used for background.

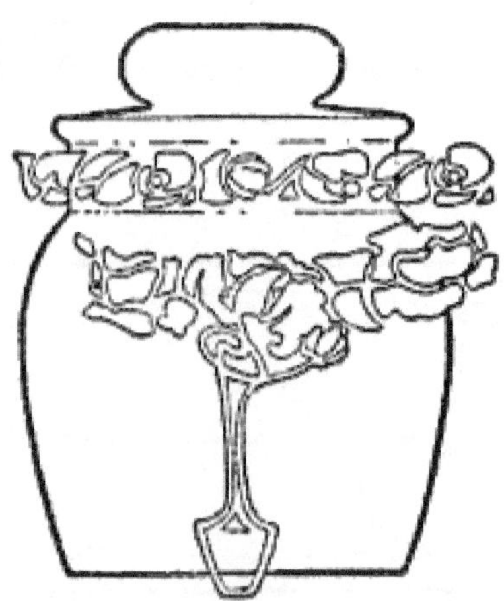

Conventional Poppies. For a cluster design the centre flower may be painted with Light Carnation, others with Sweet Pea Pink. Poppy Red and Yellow Red are also suitable tints. Stamens should be painted with Black or Violet mixed with Black. Seed pods may be painted with Gray Green tipped with Black. Leaves and stems may be laid in with Apple Green shaded with Shading Green. For background use Oriental Ivory mixed with touch of Black. For lustre decoration use Rose Lustre for centre flower and a thinner application for outside flowers. Seed pods may be Gray Green painting color and stamens Gold. Leaves may be painted with either Light Green Lustre or Apple Green painting color. Stems should be the same. Background of Mother of Pearl Lustre or Oriental Ivory painting color.

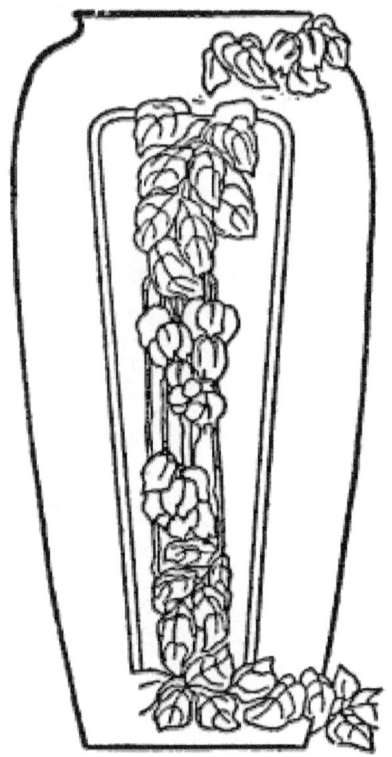

Bittersweet. Some of the berry forms Yellow-Red, others Albert Yellow mixed with Pompadour. Moss Green is a very good tint for upper leaves and Apple Green mixed with a touch of Deep Purple for lower leaves; a touch of Black may be added to this mixture for darkest leaves. Auburn Brown should be used for stems. Background of Oriental Ivory mixed with a touch of black is effective for such an arrangement. If the design is a panel effect bordered with bands, Gold may be used to good advantage for bands.

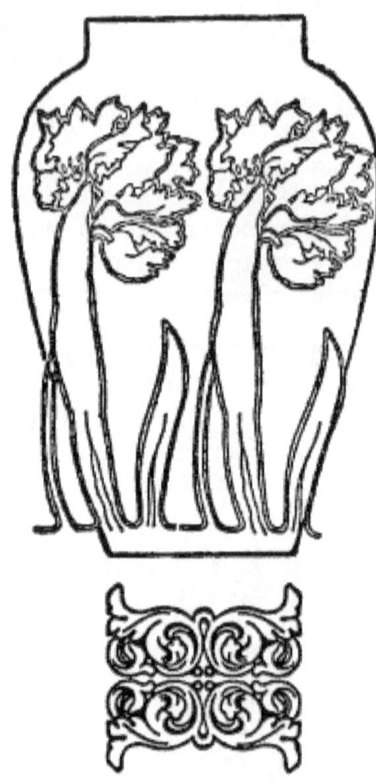

Tulips. If the design be a cluster, the larger flowers may be painted with pale Primrose Yellow shaded with Yellow Green at base. If any petals turn or curl back into the background these may be laid in with Violet of Iron. Sweet Pea Pink and combinations of White and Pink (striped) may be used with good effect for other flower forms. Stamens may be painted in with black. For leaves use Yellow Green or Gray-Green at top, shaded into Royal Green, and at base use Shading Green. For background use Royal Copenhagen Gray from a very light tone at top shaded into deeper tones at bottom.

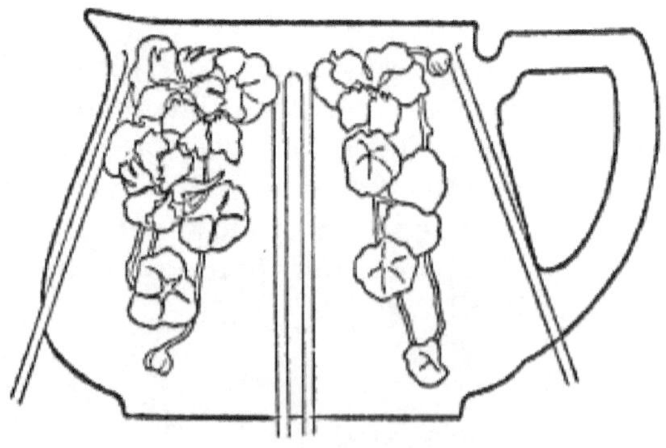

Nasturtiums. This popular motif may be painted in a great variety of color schemes. For Yellow flowers use Primrose Yellow (various shades). Ivory Yellow and light application of Yellow-Brown. Pinks and Blood Red may be used for other shades and mixture of Blood Red and Auburn Brown for Mahogany shades. Light leaves may be laid in with Apple Green mixed with Gray Green and deeper ones with a mixture of Apple Green and a touch of Deep Purple. Moss Green mixed with Gray-Green is also a good combination. For background use Auburn Brown next to the design, blended into Oriental Ivory.

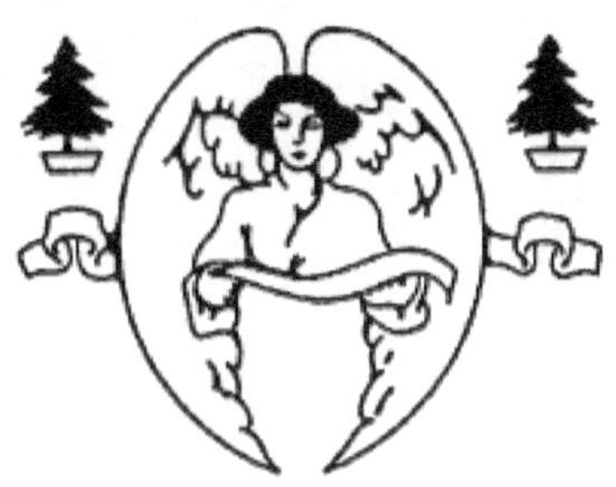

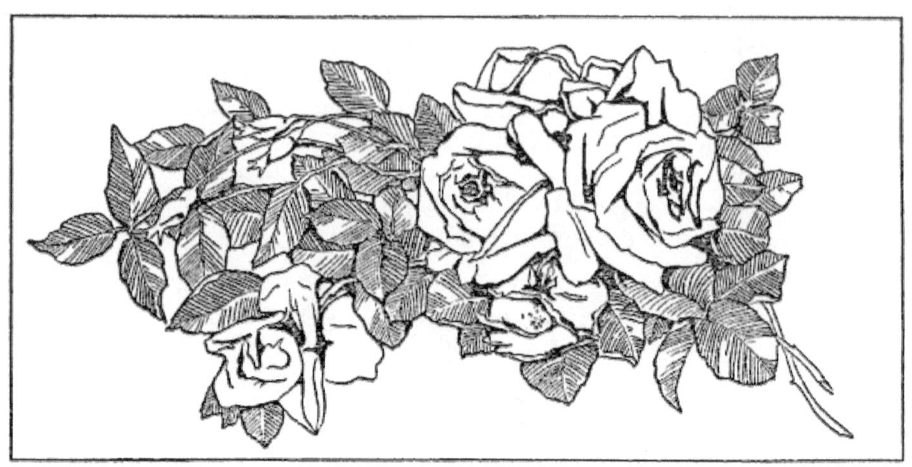

FLOWER PAINTING

It would be impossible in this small work to go into detail of this subject, considering the number of flowers we would have to deal with—consequently we will deal only with the most popular subjects. When painting an American beauty rose, paint the center and shadows in crimson purple, mixed with about one-sixth part of darkest green. The half shadows are done in crimson purple, leaving the lighter parts white. Use colors of medium thickness. The piece is then ready for the first firing.

Next go over the light parts with American beauty color, but treat the shadows with crimson purple. Be especially careful about keeping the shape of the rose as true as possible. Use crimson for the detail work of the petals. Fire the second time.

If a third firing seems necessary, retouch, using the same colors.

When very delicate shades are desired, in rose painting, a light dusting of brown-green toward the centre will prove effective. Some of it can be dusted over the background. This should be done before the second firing. The centre of a rose should always be a pure rose color. If colors are applied too thickly, they are sure to chip off. It has been learned by experience that dark greens are the most satisfactory to use with purple or ruby when dark effects are needed. Blacks and browns mixed with purple usually oxidize.

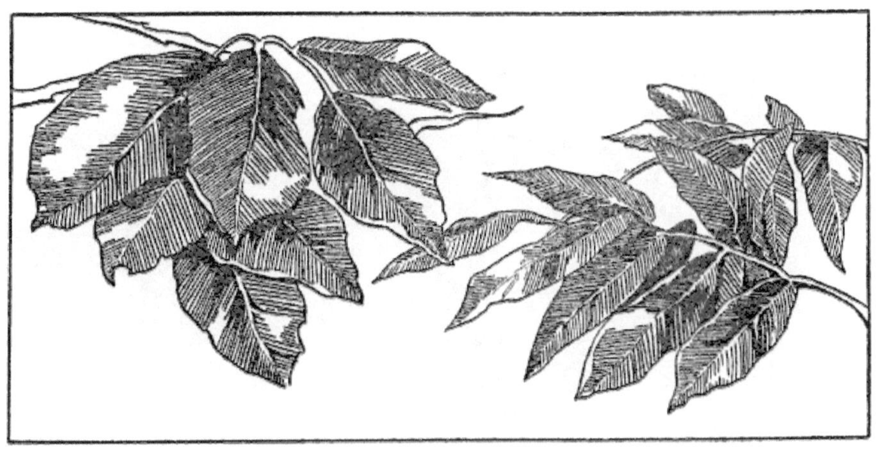

LEAF PAINTING

The average artist pays too little attention to the foliage in flower painting. He starts out to paint a flower and the leaves seem like a secondary consideration. Any handling is often thought to be good enough. This is a great mistake, as the treatment of the leaves may be the making or marring of a decoration. Many people are of the opinion that they are very easy to paint. This is another mistake. They are just as difficult and require as careful handling as the flowers or fruit itself. It would be very hard to give definite instructions on this subject. The many varieties with their various beautiful edges and veinings, need individual handling, just as much as flowers do. The shape of the article on which the decoration is placed, has much to do with the handling.

There are, however, a few rules that will generally apply.

Leaves must present a crisp appearance. To accomplish this, the color should be applied with as few strokes as possible. All detail work must be left for the second firing. Large regular leaves can be completed with two strokes—using the dark color for one and lighter color for the other.

The student should aim to make irregular leaves as simple as possible. It stands to reason, however, that more strokes will be necessary for these than for regular ones. In china painting, lights are supplementary. It is the shadows that give real character to the subject. These should be fired first, and the lights second.

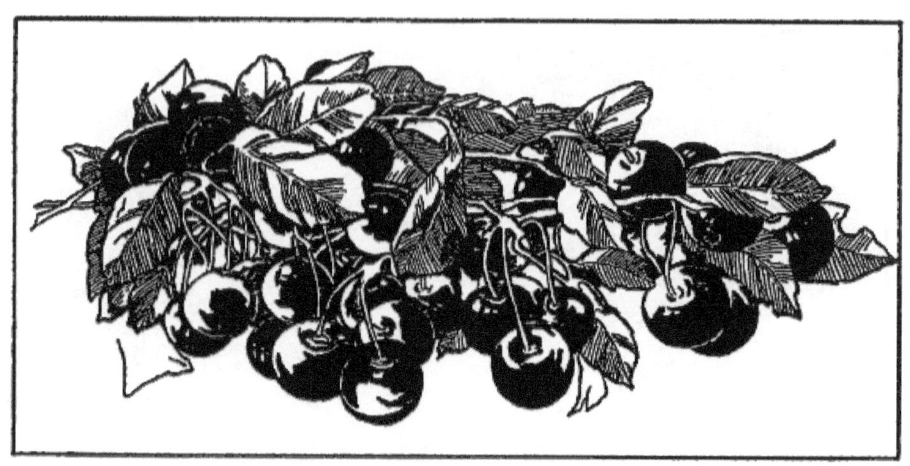

FRUIT PAINTING

One of the important points of fruit—and flower painting as well—is the proper form of leaves. Some decorators fall into the habit of painting leaves of blackberries, currants, grapes, plums, etc., all in the same irregular and ragged manner for which there is no excuse other than lack of experience or painting leaves from memory. Above all we advise the student to study the different leaves carefully. There is such a variety of fruits and flowers that volumes could be written in describing them, so we will confine our efforts to instructions on painting the fruits most commonly used as designs for china painting. These are blackberries, cherries, currants, plums, grapes and a few other varieties. *Blackberries* and *wild cherries* are laid in with a wash of black for the first firing, which should be applied only on the dark side of the berries. The light part and the highlight should be left pure white. For second firing, apply a wash of banding blue and black with a little purple added to give it warmth. Wipe out one or two sharp highlights just above center of berry to give it fullness and transparency; the piece is then ready for second fire. Should a third fire be required, be careful not to use too much black as dark colors are apt to blister if applied too heavily.

Another combination for a beautiful dark color is first apply a wash of dark green over the dark part of the berry for first firing and going over it with a wash of crimson purple for second fire. You must not omit wiping out highlights which are especially noticeable on fruits with smooth skin.

Red Cherries. For painting red cherries, use dark pompadour for the dark parts and poppy red for the lighter portion. Violet or iron is a good color to use for deep cherries.

Currants. For currants, dark pompadour is a good color to use, but it should be kept thin and the highlights must not be forgotten. Currants of a lighter red may be painted with poppy red.

Plums. Crimson purple and banding blue are used in painting plums—about three parts of blue to one of crimson purple. This same combination may be used for second firing, with a light wash of black for deepest shadows.

Grapes. For painting dark blue grapes, use a mixture of about two parts banding blue to one part each purple and black. A strong contrast between light and shade should be an essential. Red grapes are treated the same as those above, but here violet of iron should be used for shadows, and dark pompadour mixed with about one-eighth part ruby for lighter portion. These applications should be applied very lightly.

Green Grapes. Shadows of green grapes should be laid in with a light wash of olive green. The light parts are left white. A delicate stroke of egg yellow around the under side of berry will give transparency to the fruit. The reddish tones may be added with a mixture of poppy red and pompadour for second firing.

Strawberries. It will be noted that dark pompadour is a very useful color for fruits. The shadows in the strawberries should also be laid in with this color and the light parts with a very light application of light pompadour. It will not be amiss to remind the decorator that in china painting all deep shadows are painted in for first firing and the lighter tints applied for second and third firings.

Crab Apples. Paint in the dark parts with brown green, and a light wash of yellow brown and yellow green over the light parts for first firing. Add the reddish tone with a mixture of dark pompadour and yellow red, and refire.

Oranges. Oranges are usually painted with yellow brown. Shadows are obtained by laying one application over another, and blending out the color thinly for lights.

Red Raspberries. These are laid in with dark pompadour for both light and dark parts.

Gooseberries. Lay in the shadows of the tints with moss green and apply wash of apple green over the light parts. Ripe gooseberries have a pinkish cast. To obtain this tint, a light dusting of peach blossom over a very light application of light pompadour will produce a delicate pink, very suitable for this purpose.

Peaches. The greenish cast in the outer edge of dark shadows of peaches, is laid in with brown green. This color should be blended with the light parts with a wash of bluish violet color. For the pink tones of the fruit apply a light wash of dark pompadour and the painting is ready to fire.

For the second firing, paint over the entire fruit with a mixture consisting of one part of yellow brown and two parts of ivory yellow. Then strengthen the reddish tints and the shadows.

Do not attempt to work too fast by using the colors too thick. China colors should be used sparingly. The strength of tints is obtained by frequent firings.

Flowers or fruit painted with repeated applications of color will appear soft, glossy and transparent.

"Dusting of colors," which has been treated under separate heading, will be invaluable in obtaining the delicate blendings so necessary in all natural styles of decoration.

After fruit and grounds have been painted, light dusting of powder colors such as delicate yellow browns, greens and light pinks may be applied with cotton rubbing lightly over fruit and background to produce a soft, harmonious relation of tints.

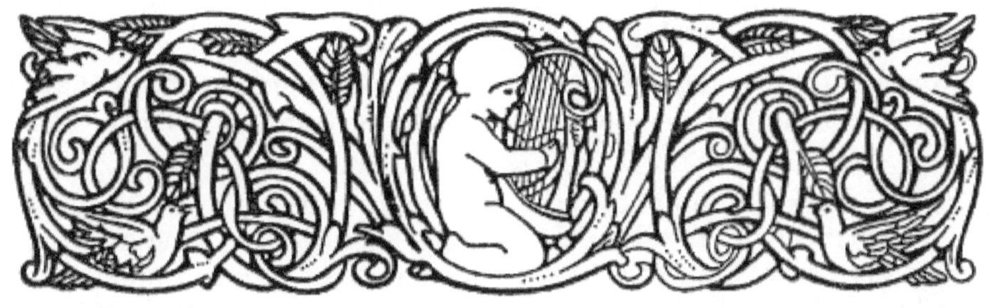

FIGURE PAINTING

The art of figure painting is somewhat difficult compared with the other styles of china decoration, and has been made more so by the introduction of many unnecessary colors and methods of applying them. The beginner who has tried to follow these complicated methods has become discouraged in this very interesting and valuable art of china painting. Figure painting on china has been greatly admired and if a simplified and understandable method were taught, it would become one of the most popular styles of decoration.

Egyptian, Greek, Roman and Renaissance decorations of pottery are all very beautiful, and in these we find figures as the motif, painted both in conventional and in natural style. These decorations do not seem to have been generally followed, although quite easy to produce. But in this chapter we will consider flat figure painting. This being supplementary, it will be found to be the easiest way to produce figures in their natural colors.

In this work, the first requisite is to have the drawing on the china absolutely correct. This can be traced from a drawing on paper on to the vase and special attention should be paid to having clean cut, perfect lines.

In handling the subject of flesh tones we will speak first of the face, and by the use of the same process, all flesh colorings, even full nudes can be painted.

Having drawn the features as lightly as possible, outline them with flesh shadow very lightly. Then proceed to the shadows of the face. These must be done very smoothly with the same color. On the edge of the shadow add a little flesh gray toward the lighter part of the face. This neutral tone, between the light and shadow, is seen on a person with a good clear complexion. These colors should not be mixed but blended well and carefully. The gray should be a pure tone although very light, as the figure will be spoiled if it is too heavy, for in firing it will be inclined to turn green. Outline the lips faintly with flesh tint and in the same way apply the color desired for the eyes and hair. To be explicit we would say that flesh shadows and flesh gray only are used to paint a face—and the lights left white. All the work must be done while the colors are fresh, and done smoothly so that they will be well blended. If these details have been carefully observed—the article is ready for firing.

To prepare the decoration for a second firing wash the face all over with a light coat of flesh-soft-tint and then touch the shadows with flesh shadow, while the wash used is still moist.

The gray tone should not be used a second time as the first application will show through the flesh tint as a soft warm gray. Retouch and strengthen wherever it is found necessary, and cover the lips with a touch of flesh-soft-tint. Remove all the little high lights, and the article is ready for a second firing. Pay attention to this suggestion. For first firing always use flesh shadow and flesh gray and for second firing use flesh shadow and flesh-soft-tint.

For third firing, shadows should be touched up with flesh shadow; touch up the cheeks with a light application of flesh-soft-tint, and use the same color to shade the lips. Hair, eyes, etc., may be now finished and the piece fired.

It is plain from this short explanation that a method of figure painting could not be more simple and productive of good results. The student is not apt to become confused when only these flesh colors are used.

Flesh gray mixed with flesh-soft-tint makes a darker tone, suitable for shadows of the eyes, etc. Flesh shadows may be added to the above mixture. With a little practice it will be found that by this method of figure painting satisfactory results are obtained in a very short time. The following suggestions should be observed when painting hair for faces of light complexion: Apply a wash of flesh shadow, for shaded parts only, for first firing, leaving the lights pure white; for second firing, a wash of yellow brown should be applied over both light and dark parts and the shadows retouched. Dark hair is painted in the same manner, using hair black softened slightly by adding one-sixth part banding blue. Flesh gray is used for painting gray eyes, and finishing brown for dark eyes. Chestnut colored hair is painted with hair brown or finishing brown. The various colors for painting hair as treated above may be mixed with other colors to suit the preferences of the artist.

It is well to remind the decorator here that the one great fault that the artist has to guard against is, using too strong a red for faces. Use flesh tones and light grays sparingly and bear in mind, never use yellow as it produces a disagreeable effect. Nude figures are painted according to the same methods as explained for painting faces. Brunettes require stronger shadows and grays, but the flesh-soft-tint is used for both light and dark complexions.

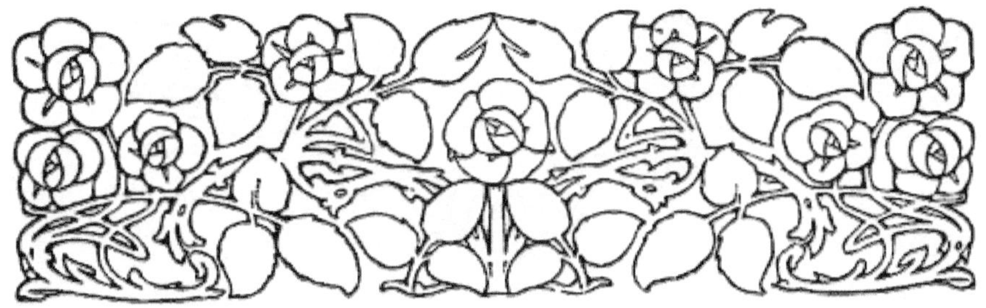

TINTING

In tinting china, the best results are always obtained by using freshly mixed colors. They work more easily and smoothly. A broad tinting brush or square shader should be used for this work—one color or a combination of colors may produce a tint. Apply the color as smoothly as possible, but if it is found to be not quite even, pad it with a cloth or pad. Some colors contain more grit than others—and are more difficult to pad. In applying such colors as yellow-brown, brown-green, apple-green, dark pompadour and pink, it is necessary to dampen the pad with mixing oil. When using the smoother tints, it will only be necessary to tint the pad, by touching it to the color. The effect will be improved and deepened by a dusting of colors when the tint is about dry.

The term "flushing" is sometimes used when tinting is used for a background.

GROUND-LAYING

There is probably no feature in the painting of china that gives the student more anxiety than the art of ground-laying.

He is confronted by many difficulties, but when the art is mastered, feels well paid for all his work. The beautiful results are sufficient reward. A perfectly even and lustrous ground is obtained by applying powdered colors over a well padded wash of tinting oil. The results are more satisfactory than a well padded ground made of color mixed with oil before applying.

The best quality of grounding or tinting oil is the first essential. In fact it is upon this, to a great degree, that the success of the work depends. A tinted oil is usually used. Pour into a small dish the desired amount of oil. See that no lumps or bubbles are in it. Then with a clean square tinting brush apply the oil quickly over the surface to be laid with color. It is not necessary that the work should be very carefully done—but care should be taken to see that all the space is covered. Have ready for use two medium soft pads, free from lint. Pad the oil over and over again with one pad until it looks like a smooth soft tint, then repeat with the second pad. This second padding may not be necessary, but it cannot do any harm and it certainly will improve the smoothness of the oil. Here the decorator is cautioned to see that the oil is perfectly even, free from spots and scratches, as these faults would be noticeable after the color is applied. It is best to wipe off all the oil and make another application instead of trying to correct a fault on the padded oil.

After the oiled china has stood for half an hour or so, the powdered colors can be applied.

Have plenty of color on a plate and, holding the piece of china over it, take up with a piece of soft cotton as much color as it will hold, and drop it over the part of the china to which the oil has been applied. Care should be taken to hold the piece flat that is to be decorated, for if it is held upright, the color will naturally drop off. A good amount of color should be kept on the cotton while applying tint. After the oil is covered, dust with clean cotton several times. If any superfluous color remains, remove it with a soft brush.

Now turn to our chapter of cutting out. If anything of this nature needs to be done, now is the time to do it.

After firing this ground should be heavy and have a strong glaze.

By adding turpentine to the oil and mixing well a medium, heavy or light ground can be obtained. By the use of turpentine the oil is made lighter and less color adheres to it.

Sometimes the powder colors will be found hardened from packing in the vials and come out in hard pieces. Pulverize these pieces well and sift them through a cheese cloth if necessary. Various colors can be blended together beautifully on grounds by applying the lighter tint first and carrying it over slightly onto the part which is to be tinted with dark colors. In applying the darker colors use sparingly as it approaches the lighter tint and avoid leaving a sharp line. Blend the two colors together until the combination is of very smooth and soft appearance.

The more turpentine mixed with tinting oil the thinner will be the coat of powder adhering to it, naturally a lighter ground is the result. For purple, violet color, maroons and pinks use light oil for grounds. It is difficult to remedy a scratch or imperfection on dusted grounds. If it is done with moist color and brush, bear in mind that dry powder applications fire much darker than colors applied moist with brush, and gauge the color accordingly.

For a brilliant effect, dust the unfired background with a flux or glaze. For warm colors such as browns, red and flesh tones, this is not necessary, but it will improve dark greens and blues. It is unsafe to try to paint over dry unfired grounds. To lay grounds in Matt colors, proceed in this manner. Use a little turpentine with the oil for Matt color dry grounds. These colors are opaque and it will not be noticeable if there is a slight variation in thickness in applying them. It is advisable, however, to have just a medium application.

DUSTING

In other chapters we have explained the process of dusting in underglaze work and ground laying, but the particular feature of it to be dealt with now is its use in altering and strengthening tints that have been applied with wet colors. This process is very similar to that used for underglaze work. For illustration, we will assume that you have a decoration in green or light ivory—and that you desire a warmer tint. In this case any warm color such as yellow-brown or yellow-red can be dusted on the decorations that are already dry. The color may be applied with a dry brush or piece of cotton and rubbed very gently. A small amount will adhere to the china—and thus the desired effect will be obtained. Any number of colors can be applied in this way and blended well together. Heavy grounds can be strengthened by the use of dark colors, such as browns, purples, greens and blues. While the delicate tones are softened by the use of lighter shades.

In the painting of flowers, dusting is often used to soften or darken them. This process, however, is not always confined to the flower alone, but is used to blend the rose, or whatever the flower may be, with the background. It has a very softening and pleasing effect.

In figure painting, dusting a flesh tone on the cheek will improve it very much.

An artist will feel well repaid for time devoted to investigating the many possibilities of this branch of painting, for crude and uneven work can be remedied by this process.

Gold or silver must *not* be applied after an article has been dusted in this way. The metal is usually tacky and may retain some of the little particles, and this would mar the brilliancy of either metal.

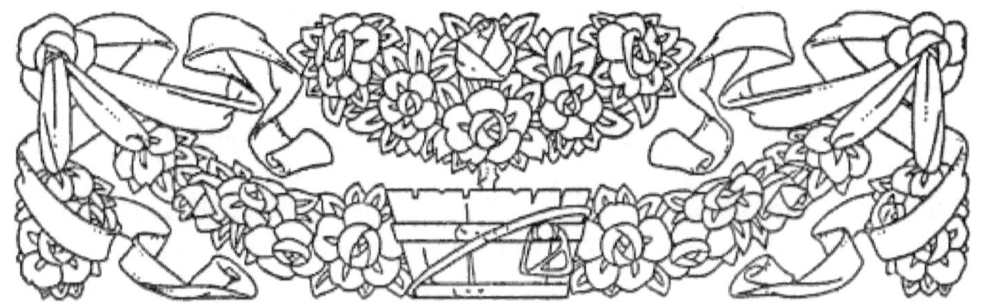

OUTLINING

For outlining china, this method—which saves one or two firings—can be used and will be found most practical.

Mix whatever dry color you wish, with water and add a couple of drops of mucilage or sugar syrup. Mix well with palette knife. Use this mixture as you would water colors—and outline the design with a lining brush. The lines will dry very quickly and in case you want to erase them, use water. Then, too, if the color dries on the palette, water should be used—and mix well. These outlines will remain perfectly, and you can paint and repaint over them—there being no danger of rubbing off and will show through oil mixed colors.

If the background is applied with regular mixed colors—and the design cut out and tinted, you can have a piece of decorated china complete with one firing. The outlines will fire clearly, but if outlined in India ink they would have disappeared.

When this method of outlining is used, a brush should be used instead of a pen. When using a pen in outlining, mix the colors with mixing oil—to about the consistency of that would be used in painting. Dilute this sufficiently with diluting medium, so that it will flow readily from the pen. Experience will soon teach you the right consistency. It is just as undesirable to have it too thin as too thick.

For small lines use a fine pen and a coarse one for heavier work. A small brush can be used successfully.

India ink is used for outlining china for decorating. This disappears in firing. It does not injure the gold or colors—but the ink lines can be seen when lustres are applied over them. When the ink is perfectly dry, the china colors can be applied.

To make a broad outline, paint the line with grounding oil that has been mixed very well with a small amount of lampblack. Draw the lines, then dust the powdered color over them. You can be sure of obtaining a perfectly even color effect, if the banding is done in this way. When outlining with gold, use a mixture of pure Roman gold and diluting medium. When mixed with a diluter, Roman gold may be applied with either a pen or a brush. Do not use turpentine or liquid bright gold.

Burnish silver can be handled in the same way.

When using liquid bright gold or lustre, you can use a brush or pen, whichever you choose.

Outlining in color can be done over fired colors, golds, silvers and lustres, but be careful not to apply it too heavily or it will flake off.

You can outline in color over unfired dry tints and unfired, well dried Roman gold. The powder must be mixed with water when used over unfired lustres. The lustres would be spoiled if turpentine or oil was used as they spread too easily. The best thing to use in gold outlining is diluting medium with powder gold, but lavender oil is very good.

CUTTING OUT

Sometimes it is necessary to wipe out a design from a background. In this case the following suggestions are recommended:

The design to the "cut out" must be seen from underneath the tint. A design to be wiped out of a tinted background must necessarily be drawn in with India ink. For dusted grounds the oil should be wiped off the ink lines with a pointed stick so that the tint will not adhere to the line.

Dusted backgrounds require about twenty-four hours to dry, but by artificial heat the time is considerably shortened. To remove the tint covering the design, make a mixture of oil of cloves and a few chips of soap. Apply a light coat and be careful that it does not spread beyond the lines. The color requires about five minutes to soften and may then be removed with a piece of cloth over the finger tip. Do not try to remove the tint until the design is perfectly dry. Use care in removing the color so as not to drag it over onto the background, change cloth frequently so that you are constantly working with cloth free from oil and color.

Designs may be "cut out" from powdered background by using a stick and scraping off the tint. It should be done while the tint is still fresh. The former method, however, is more satisfactory, tar oil may be used instead of oil of cloves if preferred.

PADS AND DABBERS

To help in the making of even grounds, pads and dabbers are used. They are also used for flushing combined colors. These can be made of any soft material, such as cheese cloth, silk, etc. The softer the material is, the more satisfactory the work will be. A medium hard ball of cotton can be covered with the material and used for this purpose. Be sure to see that the material is without wrinkles. Singe all lint off of the dabber with a lighted match. In padding color dab quickly and lightly, working the tint evenly by light, gentle tapping. A silk dabber is more desirable and there is no better material for the purpose than an old handkerchief or any soft piece of silk that has been frequently washed. Fine cheese cloth will do, especially on heavy grounds.

Cheese cloth will permit the cotton to absorb some of the oil and it does not retain much of the tint. Professional decorators of china use this method in tinting. Color should not be padded while very fresh as a large part of it would be taken up by the pad. More satisfactory results are obtained by allowing the tint to become slightly "tacky" before padding. For best results in spreading heavy tints, fitch hair stippling brushes or dabbers are used before using cloth pads.

If the pad produces an uneven or grainy effect, rub the superfluous color from it with a piece of paper. Moisten the dabber lightly with oil before proceeding with the work. When tinting with banding blue, yellow-brown, grays or pinks a little more oil should be applied to the pad. Fine cotton or lamb's wool are suitable for making pads.

SLOW OR QUICK DRYING COLORS

Almost every student experiences difficulty, at times, with the uncertainty of colors drying in the way desired. Sometimes they will dry too rapidly and at others not fast enough.

It is well to use diluting medium to keep the colors moist, but use a regular mixing medium with colors. Oil of lavender is not practical as it dries quickly. Mixing oil is too thick.

Slow drying colors are essential in painting broad grounds. Very often time is needed for changes in designs. It is always necessary to have something to moisten the brush with while working—any diluting medium can be used then. Only a very little is necessary and no other oil *need* be used. For very slow drying add a drop or two of oil of cloves when mixing the colors. Naturally, the colors will remain moist according to the amount used. Should too much be used, the colors will run. Sweet oil is also used, but less should be used than of the oil of cloves or the colors may remain moist for several days.

Turpentine or oil of lavender are the mediums used for quick drying. Colors will dry quickly and thoroughly, if a little turpentine is added and mixed well with the colors that have been previously well mixed. To dry colors or keep them from running, a little steam will be effectual.

Perhaps it will be only necessary to breathe on the surface.

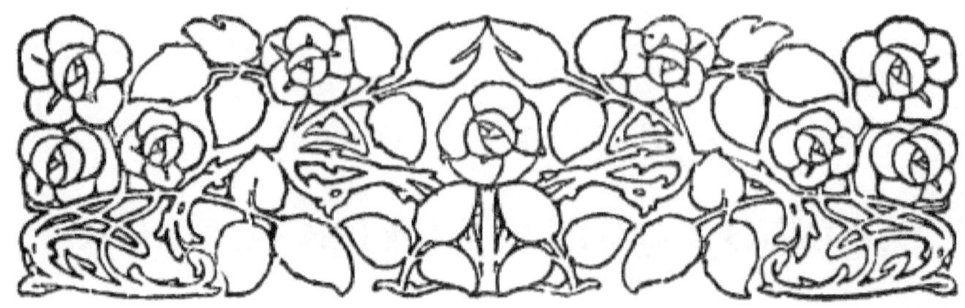

PASTE OR RELIEF WORK FOR GOLD

The beginner is confronted frequently with two difficulties in paste decoration. These are flattening of the paste after the application, and chipping off. These can usually be traced to one of two things: the use of the wrong quality of oil or to using too much.

Unsatisfactory results will always be obtained if the paste is insufficiently ground. It is well to grind it well with turpentine. Allow it to dry, and then mix with oil—a horn or steel knife can be used.

Some of the professionals who do the finest work for the English and French manufacturers, mix their paste with two parts of fat oil and one part of oil of tar. The paste should be mixed to a half thick consistency with the oil that is to be used, and worked until it is smooth. Special care should be taken to following these instructions.

The paste now being about like freshly mixed china colors, stir with a knife and breathe upon it. Keep stirring until it is hard and gathers to the knife in a stringy way.

Reducing the paste to the right consistency is the most important feature of the work. It should be of such consistency that when taken up it will keep in good shape while hanging to the paste brush.

If a small amount of water should be used instead of breathing upon it, great care should be used not to use too much. Too much humidity will cause the paste to become stiff.

A single long stroke produces the best results in laying paste lines. Frequent touches produces an uneven line which will mar the beauty of paste work. Be sure to lay the paste high and round like a thin cord. If it should flatten, too much oil has been used; breathe upon it again until proper consistency is obtained.

Keep paste in as small and round a heap as possible while it is being used. It is best to mix fresh paste for each day's work. If you should wish to remix paste, use as little oil as possible.

To straighten an uneven line cut the end of a brush handle to a sharp edge and smooth or move the line in place. A brush moistened with turpentine will sometimes do the work satisfactorily. Do not let the brush become clogged with paste while working. Clean it frequently by wiping it on a cloth. Dresden paste brushes are best for this work. Paste may be applied over fired colors or lustre if desired. Be sure the paste is well dried (not artificially) before firing. To obtain the best results paste should be fired before gold is applied. However, in case of emergency gold may be applied over unfired paste provided it is perfectly dry and hard.

If paste should, for any reason chip off, the space should be filled in with fresh paste. Dry thoroughly and apply gold—then fire as before. Unfluxed gold should be used over paste. For silver paste decoration, two applications of silver are necessary for best results.

GOLD

A brush used for gold should be used for that purpose only. Use turpentine or oil of lavender for moistening the brush—and after it has been rubbed well into the paste the latter will turn a thick brown color. Pour a very little turpentine on the paste if it is too dry and work well with a palette knife. A drop of liquid bright gold will soften Roman gold quickly. Don't use turpentine if you use liquid gold.

Another way (although perhaps not quite as good a way) to soften gold quickly is to warm it over a flame, then add a little turpentine. The objection to this process is, that after it has cooled it is harder—and the results are not as satisfactory.

We find in gold work, it is safe to use liquid bright gold for the first firing and Roman gold for the second. Liquid bright makes a good foundation for Roman gold and makes a good wearing combination. It is not well to use unfluxed gold on hard china as it rubs off very easily. Roman gold is used for this china and hard or unfluxed gold on the softer wares, such as Belleek.

Gold requires a medium firing—and when practical it should be applied in the last two firings. If an article that is decorated with gold requires refiring on account of some defect in the other decorations, the gold will need to be gone over again or you may have to give the piece an extra firing for the gold.

If gold is overfired it will fade white; on the other hand, if it is underfired it will rub off in burnishing.

It is very necessary to remember one thing in burnishing gold. If any of the glass fibers are allowed to remain on the decoration when the article is undergoing a second firing, they will eat the colors, and the work will be nearly if not quite spoiled.

It is unwise to burnish an article near where you are working, as the particles get into the colors and act the same when the colors are fired.

Wash each article after burnishing. After each firing of an article, burnish the gold, for handling, or moisture from the hands, or dust are sure to show. Lustres are applied after the gold is burnished.

There are many reasons for gold looking dirty. Sometimes it is due to the china being dusty. Maybe the brushes were not clean or a poor quality of turpentine was used. Gold will not stand too much mixing, consequently it is well to have only the amount needed on the slab.

After the student has had some experience in handling gold, he will probably be able to apply it over unfired paste. The paste, however, must be absolutely dry.

But the safest way to obtain the best results is to fire the paste first. Care should be taken not to apply the gold too thick or it will blister and peel off.

If liquid bright gold is used with Roman gold use no turpentine. In fact never use turpentine with liquid bright gold.

When it is found necessary to remove fired gold, it can be done with liquid china eraser.

Gold can be applied very evenly to the edges of round articles with the tip of the finger.

After silver has been fired, gold can be applied and vice versa, as one metal acts as a foundation for the other.

Mix one part of silver with two parts of unfluxed gold and you have green gold. For platinum effects mix liquid bright silver with Roman gold.

Nothing but unfluxed gold should be used with Belleek ware.

GOLD BURNISHING

The appearance of Roman gold when it comes from the kiln is Matt or dull. In order to bring out its natural brilliancy, scouring or burnishing is necessary. This can be done with a spun glass brush made for this purpose, or it can be burnished with a special sand. In case an article has to be refired, be sure to remove all of the glass fibres as they would ruin the decorations. The beauty of the unburnished gold will be destroyed by moisture from the fingers. If sand is used, moisten a soft cloth with water, and after dipping it in sand, rub the gold gently. After the gold is polished, the china can be washed. The china is underfired if the gold comes off in burnishing. The gold can be burnished more easily and more evenly if a coat of liquid gold is used in the first firing and Roman gold on the second.

LUSTRES

Cleanliness is one of the first requisites for success in using lustres. The brushes should be cleansed with Gold-Essence or Alcohol from all traces of one color before using another, and should not be allowed to dry containing any color. The corks should never be changed from one vial to another as the least contact of tints in the unfired state is liable to spoil the whole vial. The vial should be corked at once when not in use as the liquid evaporates rapidly; this will also guard against dust and upsetting.

A soft camel's-hair brush, that can be dipped into the vial, will be needed; also a wad of cotton enclosed in a piece of silk to form a pad as for ordinary tinting.

Use great care in handling pieces tinted with lustre colors. Clean the china thoroughly, using alcohol, being careful to leave no finger marks on the piece. Dust in the brush, in the kiln or on the china will make blemishes. See that the work is not exposed to any dampness. After the work is completed handle as little as possible and if necessary to be wrapped, use tissue paper, not cotton. It is best to apply the lustre in the last firings. An even tint is obtained by several applications, but always fire for each application of the lustre. A second coat on an unfired coat of lustre will produce a blotchy effect.

If lustre has fired spotty or in an unsatisfactory manner the fault can usually be corrected by applying another wash of the same color or a darker tint. A generous application of Mother of Pearl lustre will also remedy the defect. If lustre should fire too light, apply another wash of the same color and refire.

Lustres dry quickly and therefore should be padded without delay. Always have the dabber ready so that there will be no time lost after the color is applied. A good plan would be to apply lustre over a part of the surface and quickly pad it smoothly, then apply the lustre over the balance and finish by padding. To retard drying, mix a very little oil of lavender with the lustre, on the palette. This will also assist in padding the lustre more successfully. It is difficult to apply lustre smoothly with a brush inside of cups and small bowls. To obviate this pour a small quantity into the bowl and spread it with a silk dabber. Be sure that the lint has been singed from dabber. Firing of lustres require a great deal of care. The piece should be placed in the kiln in such a way that no dust can fall on it. Be careful in drying lustres as the color will pulverize if the heat is too strong. On lustre and gold decorations care must be exercised in burnishing the gold so as not to rub the lustre, as it is very easily scratched. Lustre applied too thick is liable to crack and if applied over fired color will lose its brilliancy unless the color is a very light tint. Fired tints and lustres can be removed with hydrofluoric acid.

Lustres should have a medium fire. Deep color effects are obtained by repeated applications and firings. If lustre color is to be applied over gold, see that the gold is burnished. It is not advisable to apply painting colors over lustres as the combination is not a success. Lustres applied over fired Matt colors will produce a rich metallic effect which harmonizes beautifully with gold and paste work. A variety of metallic effects can also be obtained by applying a greenish bronze tone. Ruby will produce a strong dark metallic effect, and orange over gold produces a bluish purple bronze tone. Lustres applied over liquid bright gold will be very brilliant, but richer effects are obtained over Roman gold.

Silver lustres over light fire tints will have a frosted appearance, which is very effective combined with turquoise enamels and gold and paste work. A deep, rich maroon effect can be procured by painting two coats of purple lustre over liquid bright silver. Orange lustre over ruby will produce a strong scarlet color. Orange over blue, dark green or olive, will produce greenish tints. Over iridescent rose, a good bronze tone is obtained. Over gold, it will produce a purplish bronze effect.

Yellow is generally used for mixtures with blues, greens and grays to produce lighter tones. It is a light color and is mostly used for this purpose and for backgrounds. For a strong yellow effect give several applications and firings.

A single application of light green is a greenish gray. A more intense effect results from several applications. Light green lustre is very popular as a tint used in connection with gold. That is, it is applied after the gold is fired. Rose over liquid bright gold produces a strong metallic effect. If pink or rose is overfired it will have a purplish tone. A soft pearl effect is obtained from a light wash of yellow or light green over fired rose. A background of rose is most effective for paste and gold work.

Blending of blue, pink and gray are found in iridescent rose which can be used with very satisfactory results for a background, and inside of cups and bowls. Padding is not necessary as the more irregular the tint is applied the more striking will be the effect.

Copper, dark green, steel blue and purple must be well protected from dust and humidity, or they will become spotted in firing.

Opal and Mother of Pearl will not always fire successfully. They are not, however, wholly unreliable, but have a tendency to fire off.

Yellow pearl is one of the very beautiful iridescent colors, with a variety of light and deep tones.

Two fired applications of ruby purple will make a very deep tone. It is very effective when used with paste and gold work. A fine iridescent, deep green background for gold, is obtained by firing light green over ruby.

Steel blue, as a rule, is a very pleasing transparent color, but it will sometimes fire iridescent dark greenish gray. It combines well with silver and black for conventional designs. A wash of yellow over steel blue will give an oxidized silver effect.

Copper is used successfully over gold lustre. Very pleasing combinations of colors are produced by applying enamels over unfired lustres. They assume a pinkish cast in firing.

Copper decorations on lustres are more satisfactory if the lustre is fired. It can, however, be applied over unfired lustre if it is perfectly dry. Lustre applied over India ink will fire off. Very pleasant and delicate effects are obtained by outlining with gold and pen over lustres.

MATT COLORS

Matt colors are opaque and are usually used for backgrounds, in which case they are usually applied by the dusting process, although they may be used exactly as china colors are. After being fired the surface assumes a velvety effect and looks like unscoured gold. Sometimes they are used with ordinary colors. They can be mixed with them but when used in this way they are inclined to lose some of the natural dullness. These colors will stand an unusual amount of firing without fading.

Matt colors can be mixed with white and used the same as oil colors.

If a fine bronze effect is desired, it may be had by stippling gold over fired Matt colors.

It frequently happens that after these colors have been fired, they will rub off, especially, if they have been laid on too thick. In this case make a mixture of a small amount of vitrifiable china tint and the Matt color, making a light wash, and this will fasten the ground. This wash may be blown or stippled on. It may be applied with a shader if the colors are not too soft.

Paste and gold may be applied over fired Matt colors. Roman or unfluxed gold may be used over paste, but unfluxed gold must be used if applied directly on the color.

As these colors are opaque no design will show through when fired. Consequently if any design is to be applied to these colors, it must be cut out. (See cutting out.) Vitrified china colors are used over fired Matt tints—and silver can be used over Matt colors.

These colors cannot be used successfully on such articles as table ware, as they will not stand a great amount of washing. They retain grease, etc., and would soon lose their beauty.

Matt colors are made by adding a certain amount of oxide of zinc to china colors. A little experimenting will tell the decorator what proportions to use. Grind these well together with turpentine—and dry before using. Different makes require different proportions.

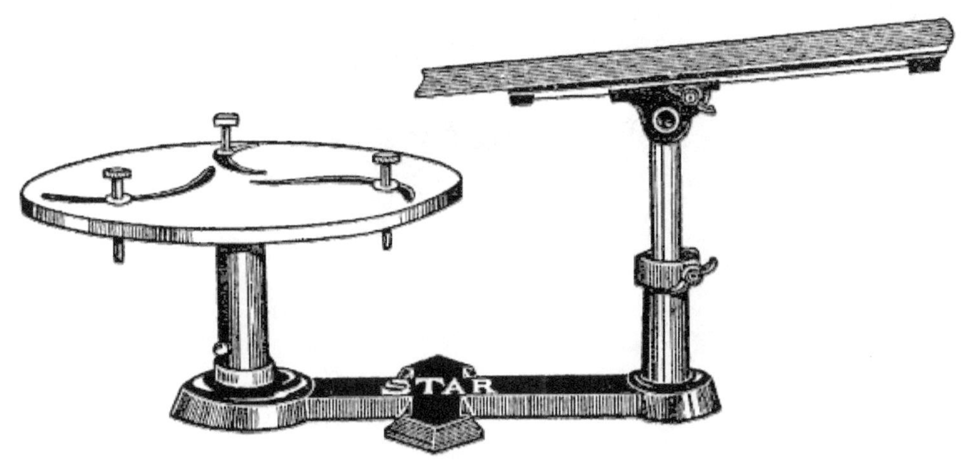

BANDING

A steady hand and practice are necessary to acquire good results in banding and lining. The best results are obtained with the "Star" Banding Wheel. Operation of the wheel is very simple. Three centering buttons move together automatically, bringing the article to the exact center and holding it in an unmovable position. These are adjustable and can be raised to hold in position bowls, vases, etc. A large amount of valuable time is saved by using the "Star" Banding Wheel. It is easily manipulated by the most inexperienced and is practically indestructible.

Do not move the brush around the china. By resting your arm on a support you can turn the banding wheel slowly and keep the brush in a steady position, and touch the china lightly.

A good brush is necessary to make a band, but a thin one is used to make a small line.

The colors must be kept in a half liquid state. In this state they flow easily and an even line is the result. The brush should pass over the same line several times.

Bands are made with grounding oil so they may be dusted with powder—the same as in the ground-laying process. This is preferable to using wet colors for a broad band. With this process the band is even and glazy. A cut liner is used for lines and edges. This brush is best for this work as it carries the large quantities necessary for a long line.

Perfect lines must be made with one stroke—as several short strokes are sure to appear blotchy. When lines are made of gold or silver, the metal used should be more liquid than when used in painting.

A compass, with a ruling pen, can be used for making lines. China color made liquid with diluting medium is used.

Lines may be drawn around the edges of bowls, plates, saucers, etc.

OXIDIZING OF COLORS

Different metals are used as a basis in producing various colors. Iron is the basis for flesh tints, reds and browns. Less iron (in proportion) is used for yellow and green.

Gold and tin are used as the basis for pinks, roses, carmines, blues, purples and violets. In mixing colors of iron basis with those of gold and tin basis the lustre and brilliancy is sometimes impaired. Experience will show that purple (which has gold or tin as basis) mixed with black or brown (iron basis) sometimes loses its glaze, on the other hand the same purple will, as a rule, keep its glaze if mixed with dark green, owing to the fact that greens have a smaller per cent of iron. The combining of the two basic metals causes the oxidization, and this difficulty is hard to remedy. A scroll of gold or silver is quite a help in this dilemma, they being opaque, defects are easily covered. Satisfactory tints can be procured by mixing colors of iron basis as one class and those of gold and tin basis as another.

A piece of china will sometimes come from the kiln with a perfect glaze, but soon loses its lustre and becomes Matt. This may be due to the fact that the color is too heavy and not fired long enough.

The china being porous absorbs the natural moisture in the air and appears to be oxidized. This can be removed with soap and water. Refiring will prevent a recurrence of this condition.

Special care should be taken with such colors as purples and browns, that too much oil is not used in mixing. It has a tendency to produce a dull, undesirable appearance. Keep the colors as dry as possible.

GLAZING OF UNDERFIRED COLORS

Even though every precaution known to the art has been observed, the artist will be puzzled in taking from the kiln pieces that have been fired in a way anything but satisfactory or as he expected. It is frequently the case that his best pieces are underfired. Knowing the danger of *over* firing, he is liable to make this mistake. Should this happen, it is not well to refire china without going over the work with a thin coat of color. This should be fired at the same heat as would be used in the ordinary glaze. In case you do not need to go over the whole decoration, the fired colors could be covered lightly with a coat of enamel oil, or mixing oil and turpentine. Let this coat dry, padding it well, after which dust it with white flux or ivory glaze. The desired glaze will be produced by the powder adhering to the oil. Fire again with ordinary heat.

A glaze cannot be produced on underfired china by using a coat of lustre, but instead it will be found that this china will absorb the glazy substance of the lustre. This has a tendency to change the colors and produces a frosted effect.

Sometimes white lustre will retain its glaze over a lightly fired tint, but we suggest that the decoration be retouched after the colors are very dry, and powder it with ivory glaze. Pure glazes or fluxes mixed with oil should never be applied over the unglazed decoration—as it will invariably destroy the colors. A rough surface can be improved by rubbing it gently with very fine emery paper.

You will find that a good oil for glazing is made by the turpentine in the cup, that you use for washing brushes. The glazy qualities are produced by the fluxes of the colors. Great care should be taken to see that this oil is clean. After giving the underfired decoration a light wash, pat well. Fire in the usual way after it is thoroughly dry, and a very satisfactory glaze will be obtained.

CHIPPING OF COLORS

There are many reasons for colors chipping, but it is probably due more frequently to the careless application of color than to any other cause.

Sometimes, and in fact quite frequently, it is due to imperfections in the china. A frequent imperfection is that the glaze is very thin and in firing the colors cannot adhere to it.

Less trouble, however, is experienced with the light colors, such as yellows, grays, blues, reds and light greens. While in the darker colors, the browns, dark greens, purples, etc., it is found that they are more liable to chip off.

Then too very hard china gives more trouble than a softer ware, such as English or Belleek.

Artists frequently think that thick colors will produce heavier tints. This is not so. The mistake is a bad one. The colors will not only chip off very soon, but will lose their brilliancy. The only sure way to meet with satisfactory results is to apply the color very evenly, avoiding lumpy strokes.

If colors are well mixed and perfectly smooth and free from grit, there is very little danger of chipping.

The most objectionable feature in china painting, and we might say hopeless one, is chipping, as there is really no good way to remedy it. The nearest thing to a solution that we can offer is to fill in the chipped place and refire—but the glaze will never be quite the same. The great danger in refiring is that some other part of the decoration may be marred in the same way. Whenever the chipping occurs in a place that can be covered with enamel or paste and gold, it is best to remedy it in this way.

One way to remedy it, and to avoid the necessity of an extra firing, is to mix the powdered color with copal varnish and apply it thickly over the chipped places. This looks fairly well and will remain brilliant for some time.

Another difficulty that may be experienced is blistering. The cause of this is bad oil. In this case the color will not chip off, but it will shrink. This condition is hard to remedy but a small amount of oil of cloves added to the mixing medium will prevent it.

In decalcomania or transfer work, blistering happens very frequently. This happens because the transfers have not been washed sufficiently, and thoroughly dried before applying. This may be prevented if a wash of oil of cloves is used, over the dry transfer, dabbing it on with a slightly moistened pad. It is absolutely necessary that the transfers should be free from any trace of moisture.

ENAMEL WORK

One of the most essential features in this work is to have the enamel of the right consistency. There are many good enamels in the market but we have found that Aufsetzweiss in tube or powder form, makes a very satisfactory white enamel.

Dilute most enamels with turpentine to a semi-fluid state. Before applying, breathe on the mixture until it is reduced to the proper consistency, which means that it should be in such shape that it can be applied in a long, free stroke. At the same time it should be thick enough to lie high and round on the china. The beauty of the decoration depends on this feature. Considerable of experimenting on the part of the student will be necessary in order to perfect himself in this work. Enamel in powder form must be thoroughly mixed with the turpentine, after which a little fat oil should be added.

Very poor work is sure to be the result if enamel is either too thick or too thin. If too thin it will be flat and if too thick it will chip off. It is about the right consistency, if it will remain in shape when a little is piled up.

When applying enamel, do not allow the brush to touch the china. Right here it might be well to advise the student that it is better to do the work over than to attempt to correct any errors by repeating strokes.

For enamelling, use a sable brush. Take up a sufficient quantity of the mixture so that some will hang to the brush. The student should aim to make high, round lines and dots. Sometimes the dots appear pointed, but after the work is fired, they will be round.

When working with enamel, it is inclined to harden. In case it does, add a drop of turpentine, breathe upon it and it is ready to use again. Sometimes enamel will chip in firing. In this case scrape it off and apply again.

Enamel that is too oily will chip—so it should be dried with a piece of silk. There are other causes for enamel chipping. Too many firings and insufficient mixing will cause it. Enamel should not be fired more than twice. Do not use it unless freshly mixed. There is little danger of these colors chipping off of Belleek or any soft glazes. Enamels are not likely to chip, if it is allowed to dry well before firing, provided that all the suggestions in this chapter have been observed.

A good tinted enamel can be produced by adding one-fifth part of the color to four-fifths of white enamel and mixed very thoroughly. These colors dry darker than when applied—so they should be mixed accordingly. Blue, green, pink and ruby produce good colors—but reds and browns do not.

Another method is to tint white enamels by washing lightly with color. White enamels can also be applied over unfired colors or fired gold. If used over unfired lustre colors it will turn reddish. White enamel fires very well though, over fired lustres.

Flat enamels are produced in a slightly different way from the raised enamels. Mix the white enamels according to the directions given before—and add to it one-fifth of the color to be used and one-eighth of flux. This is then diluted with oil of lavender. Use sufficient to reduce it to a fluid state—and mix well, a square brush is the best for this work. Let the enamel flatten itself naturally. After this is fired the ground appears higher.

One firing is all that is needed for flat enamels.

When several flat enamels are to be applied to one article, the greatest of care should be taken to see that one color does not run over the other. They should be separated by heavy lines—and each one dried.

Peach blossom or ruby are used for pink enamel. Albert yellow for yellow, peacock or Russian green for green and blue green, or turquoise blue for blue. Some colors that cannot be produced are bought prepared ready for use.

Enamels should not be fired heavily. Add one-sixth of china cement to enamels and you have an excellent filling for cracks and nicks in china.

Glass enamels give better satisfaction when mixed with water rather than oil. Mixed in this way, the danger of chipping is reduced to a minimum. These enamels are made by mixing Matt colors with white enamel. Handled in this way the enamels seldom bubble.

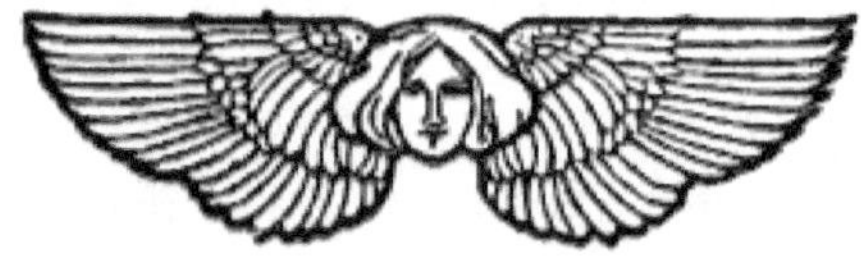

CHINA REPAIRING

To repair a piece of china that has been cracked through and through, use "cement to be fired," mixed with water, until nearly liquid. Apply it to the crack repeatedly, so as to let the china absorb as much of it as possible; then wipe away all the surplus, and fire. This cement contains quite a good deal of flux, and will affect any color covered with it. It will always prove satisfactory when applied nowhere except just inside of the cracks.

If the article to be repaired is broken into many pieces, tie them together with asbestos cord before applying the cement to be fired, and fire with the asbestos. Asbestos will not leave a mark on hard china, and only a slight one on Belleek ware; but even this can be prevented by firing very lightly, and the cement will be quite as effective.

It must be remembered that this cement has no body and will do nothing toward filling in a space; it melts completely and holds the pieces together. If the crack is wide, apply the cement first, as explained before; let it dry, and then fill in the crack with enamel mixed with either oil or water.

To imitate the color of the decoration through which the crack comes, add a bit of the desired color to the enamel, being careful to remember that tinted enamels are rather darker after firing than before.

Fill in a nick with enamel mixed with one-tenth of flux. After this is fired, it may be covered with paste and gold, and the fault will be completely obliterated.

By mixing one part of flux to nine parts of very finely grated china, a good filling will be produced for large cracks, or for places from which small pieces of china are missing. It must be very carefully applied, and dried before firing.

Paste and gold work will cover up cracks very nicely.

Unless the china is actually apart, the cement need be applied to only one side.

For a cracked vase, apply the cement by letting it run along the inside of it only, but on a platter, apply it on the outside, or, if desired, on both sides.

Black spots and pin holes can be filled in with enamel.

China can also be repaired by using a cold cement, which should not be fired. Apply the cement with a stick, on the edges of both pieces, and put them together very carefully. Set the china aside, so that it will remain undisturbed until dry. If there are many pieces, join two or three, and let them dry, and gradually add on the others until the article is complete. Allow two days for an ordinary good drying, without artificial means, before handling.

A strong cold cement is made by mixing two parts of cheese to one part of powdered lime, adding water until the mixture is of a semi-liquid consistency. Mix and grind it with a knife until it has become tacky. Apply this to the edge of the china, and join the pieces carefully, allowing one day for it to dry.

Many large crockery houses use this cement exclusively, and find it very satisfactory.

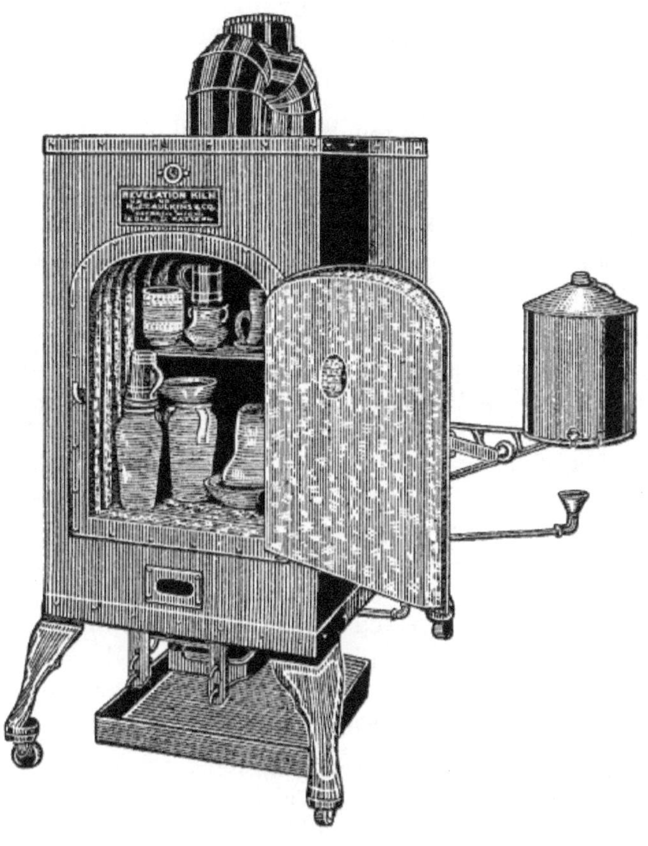

FIRING CHINA

If the kiln is raised upon a box or platform from 10 to 20 inches high, it is more convenient to stack, and also to regulate the burner. Have the box covered with a piece of zinc or sheet iron. Connect with the chimney in the most direct way, using 7 in. pipe which must not taper. If the chimney hole should be smaller, have it enlarged to this size. Set the brackets in the support upon the side of the kiln. Fill the can with kerosene oil and place upon the bracket adjusting the funnel so that the oil will drop into it. Place a small piece of asbestos fibre as large as a thimble in the iron tray in the bottom of the burner, and keep the slide in the burner well open.

Kilns are shipped with the clay in a green state in order to insure safe transportation, and must be fired in order to dry out any moisture *before* firing china.

Turn on the oil in a fast drop and apply a lighted match or taper to the asbestos fibre, which has become saturated with oil and will light. Allow the oil to flow in a broken stream for about 15 minutes. By this time the burner has become hot and will consume more oil. At first, the bottom of the pan need not be more than one-half covered, *always exercising care not to feed it too fast in the beginning*. As the kiln becomes hotter, the oil may be increased gradually and a red glow will be seen through the mica window in the door. This will gradually increase until the whole interior is red, also the flames may be seen through the mica window at the top. From this time the oil may be turned on as fast as the burner will consume it without overflowing. Usually the first time it is fired it is best to allow the kiln to run slowly for four or five hours or longer if necessary, and until it shows a good red throughout the inside, and hotter than for firing China.

The China may be stacked in any manner which is convenient. Trays and plates may be placed on edge with small stilts between, although the expert firer may stack safely on edge without stilts as long as the glazed surface of one piece is touched only by an unglazed bottom or rim of the one next. If plates are piled one above the other, it is always safer to have medium sized stilts between them. In case of a large Jardiniere, Vase, or Punch Bowl, place a large stilt beneath. It is frequently convenient to stack large pieces on the side, in which case they may be raised a little in the same way. Stack the china so that it will not wedge at any place, and so that ventilation of air may circulate about the pieces. Cups and saucers and small articles may be stacked in any possible position separated by small stilts. If you wish to use the shelves place the supports in the kiln so that they rest securely, and place the shelves upon them. Very few firers make use of them after they have become accustomed to stacking without.

It is not necessary to heat the kiln each time before firing, as moisture is not expelled from fire-brick into the oven as it is from an iron firepot. Allow the oil to flow in a small or broken stream for about 15 minutes, and then increase a little. *The main point is to feed the oil very slowly at first until the burner* has become hot, when it may be increased gradually. The first red will show in about 40 minutes. From this time on, the oil may be increased as fast as the burner will consume it without overflowing. After the interior of the kiln has been thoroughly red for some time it will grow paler in tone and a glow commonly called Sunshine will spread over it. This is the point to turn off the oil, and stop the fire. You can see whether the gold has changed color, and whether the pieces are glazed, especially any dusted tints. If your colors come out dull, and if your rose or carmines are brick color instead of a clear pink, or if your gold rubs off, you may know that you have not fired long enough. If your pinks or carmines have turned purple, you have overfired. A few trials will enable you to know for yourself, just the right length of time.

It takes from one hour and fifteen to an hour and thirty to forty-five minutes. The time varies, depending upon the draught and the way the oil has been fed.

The mistake is too often made, of firing by time entirely, instead of being guided by the appearance of the kiln. After having fired several times, one will have ascertained pretty nearly just how long their kiln takes to fire, and this time is not apt to vary greatly. Yet on some days, depending upon different conditions, it may take a trifle longer or less time, and so let your reason, rather than the clock, dictate the proper firing.

The hole under the door is intended for a peep hole, to see the condition of the fire in the combustion chamber, and should be left closed. When the chimney draft is not good a carbon may form over the burner in this combustion chamber, and by the use of a small poker through this hole it may be removed and taken out through the burner without stopping the firing.

If the kiln does not seem to respond properly, and in a reasonable length of time, you will, doubtless, find that there in insufficient draught in the chimney. This is a most important consideration, and if there is any cause, such as a stove, or fire-place connected with the same flue which cuts the draught, it must be removed. If attached to the same flue as a furnace or stove, the latter must be entirely cut off *when the fires are out in the summer*.

Sometimes it is necessary to have the chimney lengthened or pipe added to the top, especially if there are tall buildings or trees nearby. The chimney or additional pipe should not have a hood or covering of any kind. In every case, an imperfect draught is the only cause which prevents perfect success from the start. When these conditions are right, little or no carbon will be formed. If an accumulation of carbon forms in the chamber above the burner, it is because the draught is poor, and must be increased. By continuing to fire with a poor draught, you run the risk of filling the tubes and choking the kiln, which must then be cleared out before firing again, even if the draught is remedied.

After firing a few times, frequently after the first firing, small heat checks or cracks will appear in the different tubes or linings of your kiln. This occurs in all fire-brick kilns and has no serious significance. With kerosene oil as a fuel, no injurious gases are formed, and no harm will come to the most delicate ware. You may fire it with perfect safety, even if the small cracks are not filled. After a time as the cracks become larger, and seem of some consequence, they may be filled with a paste made of fire-clay and water. Do not merely plaster this paste over the outside, but force it well into the cracks. In this way the kiln will last indefinitely. Cracks are less liable to come if a little care is exercised not to cool the kiln too fast, and not to open the door while it is hot.

About three or four hours should be allowed for cooling, and in opening the door be careful not to subject the china to a sudden cool draught. Open the door only very gradually, leaving a mere crack at first, then a little larger space, etc. The sudden draught of cool air might cause the china to craze and crack.

A piece of soft glazed ware, if taken from the kiln while still too warm, is apt to show a crackled or crazed glaze, and you will hear the little crackling sound produced by the sudden contraction of the glaze.

Lector House believes that a society develops through a two-fold approach of continuous learning and adaptation, which is derived from the study of classic literary works spread across the historic timeline of literature records. Therefore, we aim at reviving, repairing and redeveloping all those inaccessible or damaged but historically as well as culturally important literature across subjects so that the future generations may have an opportunity to study and learn from past works to embark upon a journey of creating a better future.

This book is a result of an effort made by Lector House towards making a contribution to the preservation and repair of original ancient works which might hold historical significance to the approach of continuous learning across subjects.

HAPPY READING & LEARNING!

LECTOR HOUSE LLP
E-MAIL: lectorpublishing@gmail.com